GEOGRAPHY NOW

VOLCANOES

AROUND THE WORLD

JEN GREEN

WAYLAND

First published in 2008 by Wayland

Copyright © Wayland 2008

Wayland
Hachette Children's Books
338 Euston Road
London NW1 3BH

Wayland Australia
Level 17/207 Kent Street
Sydney, NSW 2000

Managing Editor: Rasha Elsaeed
Produced by Tall Tree Ltd
Editor: Jon Richards
Designer: Ben Ruocco
Consultant: John Williams

British Library Cataloguing in Publication Data

Green, Jen
  Volcanoes around the world. - (Geography now)
  1. Volcanoes - Juvenile literature
  2. Geomorphology - Juvenile literature
  I. Title
  551.2'1

ISBN 9780750254526

Printed in China

Wayland is a division of Hachette Children's Books,
an Hachette Livre UK company.

www.hachettelivre.co.uk

Picture credits
(t-top, b-bottom, l-left, r-right)
Front cover istockphoto.com/Julien Grondin,
1 Digital Vision, 4-5 istockphoto.com/Koch Valérie,
5br courtesy of NOAA, 6-7 istockphoto.com/Natalia
Bratslavsky, 7br courtesy of NASA, 8-9 James
Andanson/Sygma/Corbis, 8br courtesy of NASA,
10-11 Arctic-Images/Corbis, 10br istockphoto.com/
Vera Bogaerts, 11br (both) courtesy of NOAA,
12-13 Dreamstime.com, 12b Dreamstime.com/Anna
Palsdottir, 13br istockphoto.com/Sascha Burkard,
14-15 and 14b courtesy of USGS, 15br
istockphoto.com, 16-17 Sergio Dorantes/CORBIS,
17br Corbis, 18-19 and 19br Jacques
Langevin/CORBIS SYGMA, 20-21 all courtesy of
USGS, 22-23 Digital Vision, 23t courtesy of US Fish
and Wildlife Service, 23b Dreamstime.com/Keoni
Dibelka, 24-25 Alberto Garcia/Corbis, 24b both
courtesy of USGS, 25br courtesy of NASA,
26-27 Dreamstime.com, 26bl and 27br Tall Tree Ltd,
28-29 Dreamstime.com/Fred Stillings, 28bl courtesy
of NASA

CONTENTS

What are volcanoes?

Volcanoes are weak points in the Earth's outer skin, or crust, where gas and hot, melted rock from deep underground burst through the surface. Some volcanoes are tall, steep-sided mountains. Others are just deep cracks in the ground.

WHAT HAPPENS DURING AN ERUPTION?

When a volcano throws out red-hot rock or clouds of ash, it is called an eruption. Hot, liquid rock, called magma, wells up to fill a space below the volcano, called the magma chamber. Pressure builds up as more magma, mixed with gas and water vapour, pushes upward. Finally, the melted rock bursts through the vent, or opening, and spills out as lava. Ash, gas and steam shoot high in the air.

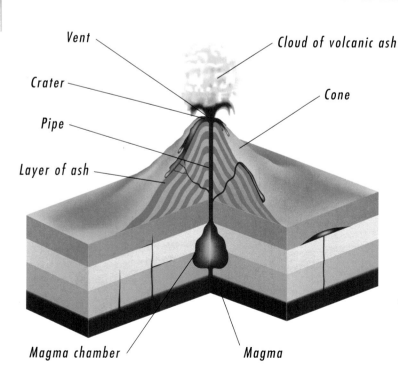

Vent
Crater
Pipe
Layer of ash
Cloud of volcanic ash
Cone
Magma chamber
Magma

Gas and water vapour mix with melted rock in the hollow magma chamber. This explosive mixture pushes up the volcano's pipe and erupts through the vent and crater.

Red-hot lava spurts from an erupting volcano, forming a lava fountain. Molten (semi-liquid) lava cools and hardens to make solid rock.

ON LAND AND AT SEA

Volcanoes erupt on land and also on the sea bed. On land, cooled lava builds up to form steep, cone-shaped peaks, or even whole mountain ranges. On the sea bed, lava piles up to form an underwater mountain called a seamount. A seamount may eventually become so tall that it breaks the ocean's surface to become an island.

Black smokers

In some oceans, scientists have discovered volcanic chimneys spouting clouds of hot water, coloured black with minerals. Water enters cracks in the rocks and is heated by the magma below. It then shoots out of vents called black smokers. The minerals in the water cool and harden to form tall chimneys.

In 1977, scientists exploring an undersea mountain chain in the Pacific Ocean discovered black smokers. Since then, the volcanic springs have been located in other oceans, too.

Why do volcanoes erupt?

Volcanoes do not erupt just anywhere. Most lie along the borders of the huge, rocky slabs that make up the Earth's crust. These sections, called tectonic plates, float on a layer of red-hot, squishy magma lying far below the surface.

MOVING PLATES

The Earth's tectonic plates are never still, but drift very slowly to clash together, move apart or graze past each other. Where plates drift apart, magma wells up to fill the gap, forming a volcano. Where plates collide, one plate moves below the other – this is called a subduction zone. When this happens at sea, the crust melts deep underground and then surges up to the surface of the sea bed, forming a line of volcanoes.

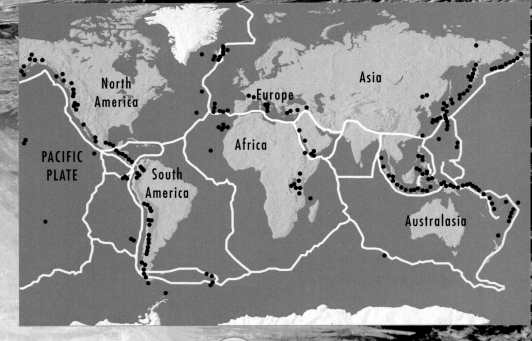

This map shows the Earth's tectonic plates, which fit together like an enormous jigsaw. Volcanoes, shown as red dots, mostly erupt on or near the borders of plates because the crust is weakest there.

VOLCANO TYPES

Volcanoes erupt in different ways, depending on the type of magma and the amount of gas inside them. Some volcanoes produce runny lava that allows gases to escape. This runny lava flows a long way before it cools, forming a low, rounded hill called a shield volcano. Other volcanoes erupt thick, sticky lava. This hardens quickly to form a steep, cone-shaped peak called a stratovolcano.

Stratovolcanoes are made of alternating layers of ash and lava. These volcanoes are usually steep-sided, but Mount St Helens (below) in the western USA is lower. This is because the top blew off in an enormous explosion in 1980.

Hot spots

Hot spots are unusual volcanoes found far from tectonic plate boundaries. They form where magma breaks through a weak point near the centre of a tectonic plate. The hot spot remains in one place while the plate slowly drifts over it. This can give rise to a chain of volcanic islands.

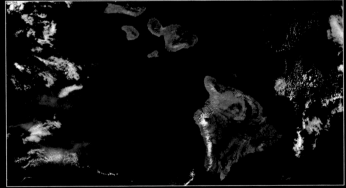

The Hawaiian Islands are a chain of volcanic islands that formed over a hot spot near the centre of the vast Pacific Plate.

Dangerous volcanoes

Rivers of glowing lava stream from an erupting volcano. Clouds of burning gases blast in all directions, and hot rocks fly through the air. Volcanoes can also trigger landslides, avalanches and deadly mudflows. Undersea eruptions can trigger powerful waves, called tsunamis, which cause great destruction.

LAVA, ASH AND MUD

Red-hot lava can engulf villages and spark fires, but lava rarely kills because it flows quite slowly. Clouds of hot ash and gas are much more dangerous because they blast outwards at high speed. Sometimes the ash is so heavy that it cascades down the mountain. These so-called 'glowing clouds' burn everything they touch. When hot ash mixes with rainwater or melted snow, it forms a fast-moving tide of mud called a lahar.

Volcanic ash is made of billions of tiny bits of rock, smashed to pieces by exploding gases. Sometimes a tall plume of ash called an eruption column shoots high in the air, as seen here from Mount Etna in Sicily, Italy.

In 1973, Helgafell on the island of Heimaey off Iceland suddenly erupted, showering ash and lava on nearby settlements. The eruption surprised the experts, who had thought the volcano was extinct.

ACTIVE, DORMANT AND EXTINCT

Scientists classify volcanoes as either active, dormant or extinct. Active volcanoes are ones that have erupted fairly recently or are still erupting. Dormant (sleeping) volcanoes may not have erupted for thousands of years, but scientists believe they will become active again. Extinct volcanoes are ones that scientists believe have stopped erupting. Some 'extinct' volcanoes do the unexpected, however – they come back to life!

Pyroclasts

Pyroclasts are all kinds of rocky material thrown out by erupting volcanoes. They vary from fine dust blasted high in the air to chunks of rock the size of houses. Rocks that are cool, and so fairly solid, are called volcanic blocks. Lava bombs are blobs of soft, semi-liquid rock that whizz through the air and splatter when they hit the ground.

Small, light pyroclasts travel further than heavy chunks of rock. Lava bombs, such as this one, sometimes twist into strange shapes as they soar through the air.

Volcanoes as habitats

Extinct, dormant and even active volcanoes can provide habitats for wildlife. Tall volcanic peaks on land are home to plants and animals that are suited to life on mountains. Out to sea, volcanic habitats include islands and seamounts. These may be colonised by anemone-like creatures and become coral reefs.

LAND HABITATS

The lower slopes of volcanoes may have a mild climate, but high summits are cold. Volcanoes often have bands of habitats, with broad-leaved forests at the base, conifers higher up, and alpine meadows nearer the top. Craters that fill with water may support aquatic plants and animals.

The Ngorongoro Crater in East Africa is the dry basin of a volcano that has become a grassland. Elephants, zebras and wildebeest (below) are among the animals that roam there.

MARINE HABITATS

Most remote islands far from land are the tops of undersea volcanoes. As soon as the volcano stops erupting, plants and animals begin to establish themselves. Plant seeds are brought by wind or water, or dropped by seabirds. In 1963, a new volcanic island rose from the sea off Iceland. Named Surtsey, it was quickly colonised by plants and birds.

The first plants took root on Surtsey just months after it emerged from the ocean. Within two years, birds and insects were living there. Scientists were able to study how quickly life arrived after a volcanic eruption.

Black smoker life

On volcanic ridges in the ocean depths, black smokers are home to many extremely unusual creatures. Microscopic bacteria thrive in the hot, mineral-rich water. They are eaten by crabs, fish, shrimps, sea urchins and bizarre tube worms. Many of the creatures that live around these vents are found nowhere else on Earth.

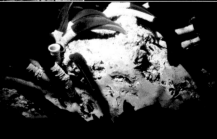

Shrimps (left) live on black smokers in the Pacific Ocean. Tube worms (below) are nourished by bacteria.

Are volcanoes useful?

Despite the dangers, millions of people live on or near volcanoes. This is because volcanoes offer rich natural resources, including fertile soil and minerals. Active volcanoes can also provide energy for homes and industry.

MINING AND ENERGY

Volcanic lava hardens to form useful rocks and minerals, such as granite and sulphur. Gold, silver, copper, tin and diamonds are sometimes found near extinct volcanoes. In Iceland and Japan, geothermal power stations use the heat of underground volcanoes to produce electricity. Water pumped underground is heated by magma to produce steam. The steam drives the station's turbines, which generate electricity.

In Iceland, people bathe in warm pools heated by volcanic activity. The geothermal power station in the background provides energy to heat homes.

FERTILE SOIL

Volcanic rock gradually wears away to form deep soil that is rich in minerals and very fertile. In many parts of the world, farmers grow crops and rear animals on volcanic slopes. In Japan, for example, rice, tea and vegetables are cultivated in the shadow of Mount Fuji, a dormant volcano that last erupted in the early 1700s.

Rice is grown on terraces dug into the volcanic soil of mountainsides throughout the Philippines.

Tourism

Volcanoes and volcanic scenery are important tourist attractions in many countries. In Yellowstone Park, USA, tourists flock to see hot springs and geysers, which spout jets of steam and boiling water high into the air.

Old Faithful Geyser in Yellowstone Park is so named because it erupts regularly, about every 90 minutes.

Predicting eruptions

Scientists who study volcanoes are called volcanologists. They try to predict volcanic eruptions. If a warning is issued, the area can be evacuated to save lives. However, it is very difficult to predict exactly when a volcanic eruption will occur.

WARNING SIGNS

Volcanoes that are about to erupt can show certain warning signs. Gas, ash and steam may leak from the crater, and the ground sometimes shakes. The sides of the mountain may bulge as magma builds up inside. Scientists can measure the temperature inside volcanoes using infra-red scanners. They can also study the history of past eruptions to work out when another is due.

This scientist is using an instrument called a tiltmeter to measure the exact shape of a volcano. Volcanoes often change shape slightly just before an eruption.

CLOSE-RANGE STUDY

Scientists use sensors to monitor volcanoes from a distance as much as possible, but sometimes close study is needed. Volcanologists wear special suits that reflect the intense heat, and a helmet or hard hat and mask to guard against fumes and flying lava. Heat-resistant thermometers are used to record the temperature of molten lava, which may exceed 1,000°C (1,832°F).

This volcanologist is taking lava samples. Minerals and gases in the sample will be studied to help work out what is happening inside the volcano.

Measuring vibrations

Volcanoes that are starting to erupt often produce minor earthquakes. Their strength can be measured using instruments called seismometers. Traditional seismometers consist of a pen attached to a weight, poised above a rotating drum of paper. The vibrations of an earthquake shake the paper while the pen stays still.

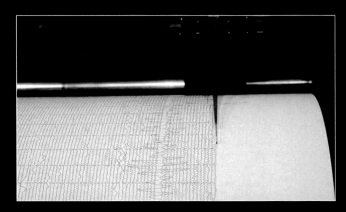

The vibrations of an earthquake show up as jagged lines on this rotating roll of paper.

Tsunami damage

Krakatoa 1883

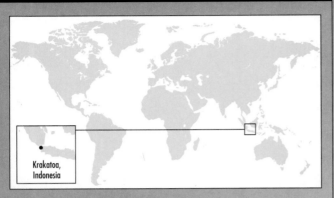

Krakatoa, Indonesia

STATISTICS

- Type of volcano: Now a caldera
- Nature of eruption: Explosive pyroclastic flows
- Death toll: At least 36,000 people
- Major cause of death: Tsunami
- Later eruptions: 1927, 1994–2007
- Current status: Active

When an undersea or island volcano erupts violently, it can cause landslides or earthquakes. The shockwaves send giant waves, called tsunamis, rippling outwards. As they race across the open ocean these waves are quite low, but they rear up in shallow water and smash on to the shore.

DESTRUCTIVE WAVES

In 1883, a volcano on the small, remote Indonesian island of Krakatoa erupted. The vent had been blocked by hardened lava. The pressure that built up inside was released in the loudest explosion ever recorded. The volcano cone collapsed, sending tsunamis up to 30 m (100 ft) high radiating outwards.

This map shows the speed of the Krakatoa tsunamis. Each coloured stripe represents the distance travelled by the waves in one hour. The volcano left a large hole called a caldera. Seawater flooded in, causing the giant ripples.

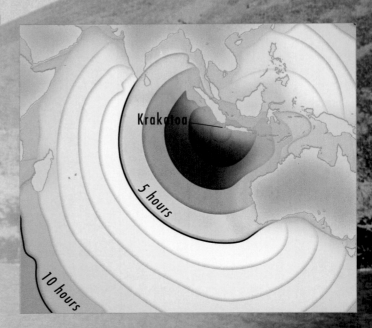

Krakatoa

5 hours

10 hours

THE RISK TODAY

The 1883 explosion destroyed two-thirds of Krakatoa and killed 36,000 people. In 1927, a fresh eruption caused a new island to break the ocean's surface. Experts fear another violent eruption may cause a similar disaster. Many more people now live in this coastal region, so the death toll could be even higher than the 1883 eruption. A system of sensors has now been built to warn of tsunamis in the Indian Ocean.

The new volcano that appeared in the caldera of the old has been named Anak Krakatoa – the 'child of Krakatoa'. It has recently started to show signs of fresh activity, releasing small clouds of dust and ash.

Subduction zone

Krakatoa lies close to a subduction zone, where one tectonic plate is diving below another. This gives rise to earthquakes and volcanic eruptions. In 2004, a major earthquake along the same fault caused tsunamis to sweep across the Indian Ocean. Over 250,000 people died.

This drawing of the 1883 eruption shows a column of ash rising from Krakatoa and raining down on the sea.

Mudflow in the Andes

Nevado del Ruiz 1985

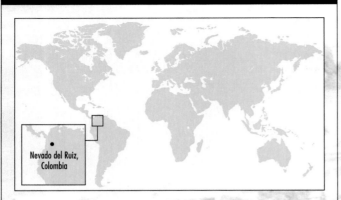

Nevado del Ruiz, Colombia

STATISTICS

- *Type of volcano: Stratovolcano*
- *Nature of eruption: Pyroclastic flows (ash and pumice)*
- *Death toll: Around 25,000 people*
- *Major cause of death: Mudflow*
- *Later eruptions: 1991*
- *Current status: Active*

This map (below) shows the lahars from Nevado del Ruiz that buried Armero, about 45 km (28 miles) from the summit.

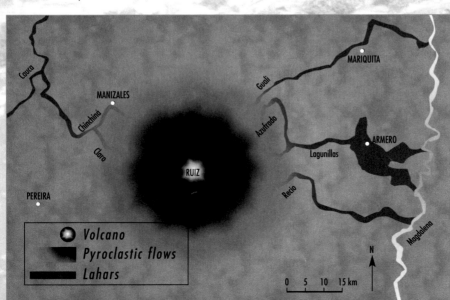

Cauca
MANIZALES
Chinchina
Claro
PEREIRA
RUIZ
Guali
Azufrado
MARIQUITA
ARMERO
Lagunillas
Recio
Magdalena

- Volcano
- Pyroclastic flows
- Lahars

N

0 5 10 15 km

Eruptions in high mountains bring added dangers. Molten lava or burning ash can melt ice and snow, producing a deadly mudflow called a lahar. This can roar downhill at high speed, engulfing towns and villages. In 1985, just such a disaster struck the town of Armero.

TIDE OF MUD

Armero was built on a plain below a snow-capped volcano named Nevado del Ruiz. The town was situated at the mouth of a narrow canyon, carved by the River Lagunillas carrying melted snow from the mountain. In 1985, the volcano erupted, melting snow at the peak. The melted water mixed with ash. A raging tide of mud and rock swept down the canyon and into Armero, killing 25,000 people.

Mud up to 50 m (165 ft) deep covers the plain where Armero stood. After 1985 the town was abandoned, but many thousands of people still live on the slopes of Nevado del Ruiz.

WARNINGS IGNORED

Armero was a tragedy that could have been avoided. The town was located on the site of previous mudflows, from eruptions in 1585 and 1845. The 1845 lahar had killed 1,000 people, but despite the danger, Armero had grown quickly. In 1984, scientists warned of the risk of mudflows, but the authorities did not take the warnings seriously enough to order an evacuation.

Rescue work

Rescue work began the day after the eruption. Emergency services found it difficult to reach the region because roads and bridges had been swept away. Rescuers struggled to free survivors trapped by the mud, which soon set like concrete. It was impossible to dig the whole town out of the hardened mud.

Victims of Armero were flown to hospital by helicopter. Some people suffered burns from mud that was still hot, even though it was 45 km (28 miles) from the mountain.

Life returns

Mount St Helens 1980

Mount St Helens,
Washington state

STATISTICS

- Type of volcano: Stratovolcano
- Nature of eruption: Pyroclastic flows (ash and gas but no lava)
- Death toll: 57 people
- Major causes of death: Landslides, mudflows
- Later eruptions: No major eruptions, but volcanic dome is regrowing slowly

A powerful volcanic eruption usually kills all life within the immediate range of a volcano, but plants and animals soon start to recolonise the area. In 1980, scientists witnessed life returning to the slopes of Mount St Helens, western USA, following a powerful eruption.

Fireweed blooms on the slopes of Mount St Helens in September 1984. Forests in the valley below are green again. In general, plants sprout more quickly in loose ash than in hardened lava.

Ash and gas shoot high in the air during the Mount St Helens eruption. The main eruption continued for four days, with several smaller eruptions following afterwards.

DEVASTATION

Mount St Helens had been dormant for 200 years before 1980, when magma started to rise inside the mountain. On 18 May, a small earthquake triggered a violent explosion. The whole north side of the mountain blew off, causing massive landslides and mudflows. The dense evergreen forests that had covered the mountain were flattened, and fallen trunks littered the slopes.

NEW LIFE

Following the May eruption, 230 sq km (90 sq miles) around Mount St Helens was an ash-choked wilderness, resembling the surface of the Moon. Yet just five months later, plants such as fireweed and lupin sprouted from the ash. As slopes turned green again, birds, insects and mammals, including squirrels and elk, returned to the mountain. Fish and frogs recolonised streams and lakes.

Regaining height

Before the 1980 eruption, Mount St Helens was a peaceful, snow-capped cone, 2,950 m (9,680 ft) high. After the eruption it was 400 m (1,310 ft) lower, but a new dome has started to rise in the crater as magma collects in the chamber below. The mountain is regaining lost height – but further eruptions are likely.

The 1980 eruption formed two new lakes in the foothills of Mount St Helens. The area is now a national park.

wildlife

Hawaiian Islands

Hawaiian Islands
Pacific Ocean

STATISTICS

- Type of volcano: Shield volcanoes
- Nature of eruption: Runny lava, lava bombs
- Major eruptions: Mauna Loa in 1950, 1975, 1984; Kilauea almost continuously active since 1983
- Death toll: 1 reported since 1900
- Current status: Mauna Loa and Kilauea are active

The islands of Hawaii are a chain of hot-spot volcanoes in the centre of the Pacific Ocean. Remote islands like these are often home to plants and animals found nowhere else. This is because these plants and animals have evolved (changed slowly) into new species, to suit the particular conditions there.

SHIELD VOLCANOES

Hawaiian volcanoes erupt runny lava that piles up on the sea bed to form rounded shield volcanoes. Only islands at the eastern end of the chain, including Hawaii itself, have active volcanoes. As the Pacific Plate bearing the islands drifts slowly west, it has carried the western islands away from the hot spot, so the volcanoes on these islands are now extinct.

Kilauea on Hawaii hurls out lava bombs that leave fiery traces. Despite appearances, this eruption is fairly gentle, and allows scientists and even tourists to get quite close.

Some Hawaiian honeycreepers have short beaks suitable for pecking seeds. Others have longer beaks that are ideal for catching insects or sipping nectar from flowers.

BIRDS OF HAWAII

The unique wildlife of Hawaii includes snails, seals and green turtles. Over 50 different species of one type of bird – called honeycreepers – are found on various islands in the group. Scientists believe they all evolved from a single species that reached the islands long ago. As the birds spread to new islands, they evolved different beak shapes to deal with the foods found there.

Highest mountain

Hawaii's two active volcanoes, Kilauea and Mauna Loa, are dwarfed by the cone of Mauna Kea. This volcanic peak is the world's tallest mountain when measured from the sea bed.

Hawaiian volcanoes are massive! This photo shows Mauna Kea, which rises 10,200 m (35,500 ft) from the ocean floor.

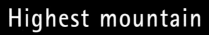

Clouds of ash

Mount Pinatubo 1991

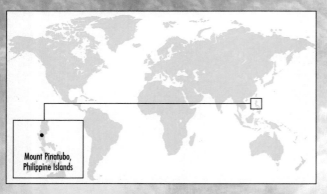

Mount Pinatubo,
Philippine Islands

STATISTICS

- Type of volcano: Stratovolcano
- Nature of eruption: Pyroclastic flows, mainly ash
- Death toll: Over 500 people
- Causes of death: Lahars, house collapse, breathing problems
- Later eruptions: Minor activity until July 1992
- Current status: Dormant

Explosive eruptions can blast huge quantities of ash into the atmosphere. As ash spreads out, it can affect the weather across the planet. The fine dust partly blocks the Sun's light, causing a worldwide drop in temperature.

CHOKING ASH

The 1991 eruption of Mount Pinatubo in the Philippines blasted ash 20 km (12.5 miles) into the air. This ash fell and covered the ground in a thick grey blanket. Heavy rain turned the ash to mud, which engulfed towns. Fine dust caused breathing problems, from which some people died.

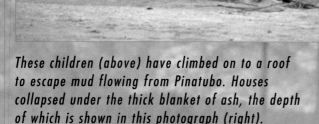

These children (above) have climbed on to a roof to escape mud flowing from Pinatubo. Houses collapsed under the thick blanket of ash, the depth of which is shown in this photograph (right).

Ash billows from Pinatubo during the 1991 eruption. The volcano released a total of 10 cubic km (2.5 cubic miles) of ash — that is ten times the size of the cloud sent out by Mount St Helens in 1980.

TIMELY WARNING

Over 500 people died when Mount Pinatubo erupted, but the death toll could have been far higher. Following warnings from scientists, all towns and villages within 30 km (19 miles) of the volcano were evacuated. Some 200,000 people left their homes. Emergency services were on full alert, and were able to react quickly to rescue survivors. This prompt action saved thousands of lives.

Spreading cloud

Ash from Pinatubo spread around the world within three weeks. By blocking sunlight, the ash caused world temperatures to fall by 0.5°C. However, this drop was small compared to the effects of the eruption of Mount Tambora, Indonesia, in 1815. This eruption vented 80 cubic km (20 cubic miles) of ash. It caused a 'mini Ice Age', with snow falling during the summer.

This satellite photo shows how gases (in red) from Mount Pinatubo spread around the world.

Tourism at Pompeii

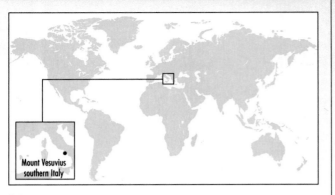

Vesuvius 79 AD

Mount Vesuvius
southern Italy

STATISTICS

- Type of volcano: Stratovolcano
- Nature of eruption: Pyroclastic flows (ash and pumice)
- Death toll: Over 2,000 people
- Major cause of death: Suffocation
- Later eruptions: Eruptions up to 1944, inactive since
- Current status: Dormant

Volcanoes that are no longer dangerous can make popular tourist attractions. One famous example is the Roman town of Pompeii, which lies below Mount Vesuvius in southern Italy. Vesuvius erupted in 79 AD, covering Pompeii with thick ash.

Public buildings and houses in Pompeii were decorated with beautiful mosaics and wall paintings. This painting shows the ancient Greek general Alexander the Great fighting a battle.

ERUPTION OF VESUVIUS

In the first century AD, Pompeii was a prosperous town. Vesuvius had been dormant for many years, so people thought the site was safe. In 79 AD, however, the volcano exploded without warning. The Roman writer Pliny described a plume of ash shaped like a pine tree rising from the mountain. Clouds of burning ash and poisonous fumes engulfed Pompeii and the nearby port of Herculaneum.

UNCOVERING POMPEII

Pompeii lay buried under several metres of ash for more than 1,700 years. Then, in the 1800s, excavation work began, led by Italian archaeologist Giuseppe Fiorelli. Fiorelli's team uncovered a well-preserved Roman city with buildings, mosaics, charred food and even the imprints of human and animal bodies intact. Millions of tourists now visit Pompeii each year to learn about Roman life and volcanoes.

Pompeii's public buildings included an amphitheatre, gymnasium, baths and temples. Mount Vesuvius looms in the background. It last erupted in 1944.

Preserved by ash

In the 1860s, Giuseppe Fiorelli invented a method of making casts of Pompeii's citizens, whose bodies had been buried by thick ash. The ash had hardened and the soft bodies rotted away. This left behind body-shaped hollows in the ash. Fiorelli filled the hollows with plaster to make lifelike casts.

Most of Pompeii's citizens died of suffocation after being swamped in burning ash and poisonous gases. Fiorelli's casting method is still used in modern excavations.

The next big one?

La Palma

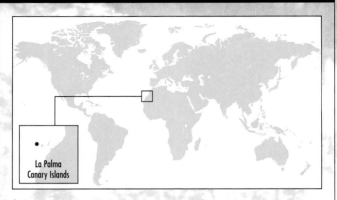

La Palma
Canary Islands

STATISTICS

- *Type of volcano: Stratovolcano*
- *Nature of eruption: Pyroclastic flows*
- *Major eruptions: 1949, 1971*
- *Death toll: one death (1971)*
- *Major cause of death: Suffocation*
- *Current status: Dormant*

Over the years, volcanic eruptions have killed thousands of people. Scientists have recently discovered several massive volcanoes (called supervolcanoes). If one of these erupted, it could cause a major disaster, such as ash clouds or tsunamis. Two possible danger sites are La Palma in the Canary Islands and Yellowstone Park, USA.

The large volcano in the centre of La Palma has caused massive landslides, but the most dangerous peak, Cumbre Vieja, lies at the southern tip, on the right in this photo.

TSUNAMI RISK

The Canary Islands are a volcanic chain in the eastern Atlantic. If a volcano called Cumbre Vieja on La Palma erupted, it might cause a massive landslide into the sea. This could send tsunamis over 10 m (33 ft) high racing across the Atlantic Ocean. In just a few hours, the east coast of North America could be flooded. Major cities such as New York, Boston and Miami would be at risk.

The hot springs of Yellowstone Park, USA, are heated by a vast pool of magma hidden below ground. The magma chamber is over 70 km (44 miles) across – the size of the whole park! Yellowstone also has geysers and bubbling mud pools.

YELLOWSTONE SUPERVOLCANO

Yellowstone Park in Wyoming, USA, is known for its volcanic activity. In the late 1900s, scientists discovered that the whole park lies on top of a vast magma chamber. If this supervolcano erupted, there would be a massive upwelling of ash and lava. Ash in the atmosphere would blot out the Sun, bringing about a sudden Ice Age. Some experts fear the Yellowstone eruption is now long overdue!

Mass extinction

About 65 million years ago, dinosaurs and other living things died out in what scientists call a mass extinction. Experts believe sudden climate change triggered their death. The cause may have been massive volcanic eruptions in India, which raised a dust cloud that blotted out the Sun, killing most plants.

Sudden climate change 65 million years ago may have been caused by volcanic eruptions or by a huge meteorite crashing to Earth, which raised a vast dust cloud.

Glossary and resources

BLACK SMOKER
An undersea volcano that spouts clouds of hot, dark, mineral-rich water.

CALDERA
A hollow that forms when a volcano's cone collapses.

CRATER
An opening in the top of a volcano through which lava, gas and ash escape during an eruption.

CRUST
The outer layer of the Earth.

ERUPTION
When a volcano becomes active and gives off ash, gas, steam or lava.

ERUPTION COLUMN
A tall plume of ash rising from an erupting volcano.

EVOLVE
When a particular kind or species of plant or animal slowly changes in order to suit environmental conditions.

FAULT
A crack in rocks, often near the edges of tectonic plates, where earthquakes and volcanoes commonly occur.

GEOTHERMAL POWER STATION
A power station that harnesses heat from volcanoes to generate electricity.

GEYSER
A hot spring that spouts a jet of steam and boiling water.

GLOWING CLOUDS
Burning, ash-filled clouds that spill down the sides of an erupting volcano.

HOT SPOT
A weak point in a tectonic plate where magma rises to form volcanoes.

ICE AGE
A period when the Earth's climate was cooler than it is today.

LAHAR
A mudflow that forms when volcanic ash mixes with water.

LANDSLIDE
When a mass of rock and soil slips away down the side of a mountain.

LAVA
Hot, melted rock from underground that erupts from a volcano.

MAGMA
Hot molten rock inside the Earth.

MAGMA CHAMBER
The hollow space below a volcano which fills with magma.

MASS EXTINCTION
When many species die out at one time.

PYROCLASTS
Any rocky material that is thrown out by an erupting volcano.

SEAMOUNT
An undersea mountain, formed by volcanic activity.

SEISMOMETER
An instrument used to measure earthquakes.

SHIELD VOLCANO
A rounded volcano formed by runny lava.

STRATOVOLCANO
A tall volcano formed of layers of ash and sticky lava.

SUBDUCTION ZONE
Where two tectonic plates are colliding and one dives below the other.

TECTONIC PLATE
One of the huge, rigid plates that make up the Earth's crust. The Earth's tectonic plates are constantly moving.

TSUNAMI
A giant wave that is triggered by an earthquake or volcanic eruption.

VENT
An opening in a volcano.

VOLCANOLOGIST
A scientist who studies volcanoes.

FURTHER READING

Experience: Volcano, Anne Rooney
(Dorling Kindersley, 2006)
Eyewitness Guide: Volcano, Susanna Van Rose and James Putnam
(Dorling Kindersley, 2002)
Jump into Science: Volcano, Ellen Prager
(National Geographic Society, 2007)
Natural Disasters: Volcanoes, Anita Ganeri
(Wayland, 2007)
Volcanoes, Anna Claybourne
(Kingfisher, 2007)

WEBSITES

www.ngdc.noaa.gov/hazard/volcano.shtml
A website from the US National Geophysical Data Center, with data on active volcanoes and major eruptions.
www.usgs.gov/hazards/volcanoes
A website from the US Geological Survey, which monitors the 170 active volcanoes in the USA.
volcano.und.edu/
A website with information about volcanoes around the world.
kids.earth.nasa.gov/archive/pangaea
A website from NASA explaining plate tectonics.

Volcanoes topic web

Use this topic web to discover themes and ideas in subjects that are related to volcanoes.

GEOGRAPHY
- Different types of volcano and their physical features.
- Why human settlements grow up near volcanoes.
- Different types of volcanic eruption and their effects.

SCIENCE AND THE ENVIRONMENT
- Plate tectonics and volcanic activity. Why volcanoes erupt on land and the ocean floor.
- How scientists study volcanoes.
- Warning signs of volcanic eruptions.

ART AND CULTURE
- Stories, myths and legends that feature volcanic activity and eruptions.
- The legend of Atlantis, a volcanic island that sank beneath the sea.
- The culture of peoples who live in volcanic areas, such as Hawaii and Iceland.

VOLCANOES

ENGLISH AND LITERACY
- Write an 'eyewitness' account of a volcanic eruption, or one from the point of view of a volcanologist.
- Debate the pros and cons of building and farming on volcanoes.

HISTORY AND ECONOMICS
- Natural resources of volcanoes, and how they are exploited by humans.
- The history of major eruptions, such as Vesuvius and Krakatoa.

Index